# SUPERSTARS OF WRESTLING

# CHRISTIAN

By Ryan Nagelhout

Gareth Stevens
Publishing

**Please visit our website, www.garethstevens.com. For a free color catalog of all our high-quality books, call toll free 1-800-542-2595 or fax 1-877-542-2596.**

Library of Congress Cataloging-in-Publication Data

Nagelhout, Ryan.
  Christian / Ryan Nagelhout.
     p. cm. — (Superstars of wrestling)
  Includes index.
 ISBN 978-1-4339-8518-8 (pbk.)
 ISBN 978-1-4339-8519-5 (6-pack)
 ISBN 978-1-4339-8517-1 (library binding)
 1.  Christian, 1973- 2.  Wrestlers—United States—Biography—Juvenile literature. I. Title.
  GV1196.C57A3 2013
  796.812092—dc23
  [B]
                                      2012029062

First Edition

Published in 2013 by Gareth Stevens Publishing
111 East 14th Street, Suite 349
New York, NY 10003

Copyright © 2013 Gareth Stevens Publishing

Designer: Nicholas Domiano
Editor: Ryan Nagelhout

Photo credits: Cover background Denis Mironov/Shutterstock.com; cover, pp. 1, 5, 13 Gallo Images/Getty Images Sport/Getty Images; p. 7, 29 Antonio de Moraes Barros Filho/ WireImage/Getty Images; p. 9, 23 J. Shearer/WireImage/Getty Images; p. 11, 17, 21, 27 Gallo Images/Getty Images Entertainment/Getty Images; p. 15 Moses Robinson/Getty Images Entertainment/Getty Images; p. 19 Gaye Gerard/Getty Images Entertainment/Getty Images; p. 25 Michael Tran/FilmMagic/Getty Images;

Printed in the United States of America

CPSIA compliance information: Batch #CW13GS: For further information contact Gareth Stevens, New York, New York at 1-800-542-2595.

# Contents

# Meet Christian

Christian is one of WWE's

biggest superstars.

5

Christian was born William Jason Reso on November 30, 1973. He was born in the city of Kitchener in Ontario, Canada.

Christian wrestled and played hockey growing up. When he was 17, he decided to wrestle professionally.

# Double C

Christian went by the name Christian Cage in his first matches. He took this ring name from two famous actors, Christian Slater and Nicolas Cage.

Christian worked his way through Canadian amateur leagues with fellow wrestler Edge. They helped one another sign with WWE.

13

# Rookie Win

Christian made his WWE debut
on October 18, 1998. He beat Taka
Michinoku for the WWE Light
Heavyweight Championship!

# Brood Brothers

Christian's early days were spent in a group called The Brood. He wrestled with Gangrel and Edge and wore dark clothes to look like a vampire.

# Tag Team

Christian and Edge teamed up often. They won their first Tag Team Championship together in 2000.

Edge

19

Christian has won a tag team title eight times. He won seven titles with Edge.

21

# Chair Champion

Christian and Edge liked to use chairs in their wrestling matches. In 2000, they were part of WWE's first "Tables, Ladders, and Chairs" match.

23

# Title Tally

Christian has won the Intercontinental and European Championships during his time in WWE. He also won the ECW title in 2009.

25

# Big Win

In 2011, Christian finally won the

World Heavyweight Championship.

He beat Alberto Del Rio in a

Ladder Match.

# Hall Bound

In 2012, Christian helped induct
Edge into the WWE Hall of Fame.
Someday, Christian will join his
former partner in wrestling's
highest honor!

# Timeline

**1973**     Christian is born William Jason Reso on November 30.

**1998**     Christian makes his WWE debut and wins Light Heavyweight title.

**2000**     Edge and Christian win first tag team title.

           Christian wrestles in first "Tables, Ladders, and Chairs" match.

**2009**     Christian wins ECW title.

**2011**     Christian wins WWE World Heavyweight Championship.

# For More Information

## Books:

Shields, Brian, and Kevin Sullivan. *WWE Encyclopedia: The Definitive Guide to World Wrestling Entertainment.* New York, NY: DK, 2009.

## Websites:

### Captain Charisma Online

*captaincharismaonline.com*
Stay up to date on any Christian news with this great fan site.

### Christian's Official WWE Page

*wwe.com/superstars/christian*
Find photos, videos, and more about your favorite Canadian wrestler.

### Instant Classic

*instant-classic.org*
This site is the leading source of information on the web for WWE superstar Christian.

# Glossary

**amateur:** a person who does something for fun, not pay

**championship:** the final game to decide a winner of a contest or sport

**debut:** a first official public appearance

**induct:** to place into something

**professionally:** doing a job for pay

**vampire:** a creature that needs to drink blood to live

# Index